The U.S. Armed Forces

The U.S. Coast Guard

by Carrie A. Braulick

Reading Consultant:
Barbara J. Fox
Reading Specialist
North Carolina State University

Capstone
press

Mankato, Minnesota

Blazers is published by Capstone Press,
151 Good Counsel Drive, P.O. Box 669, Mankato, Minnesota 56002.
www.capstonepress.com

Library of Congress Cataloging-in-Publication Data
Braulick, Carrie A., 1975–
    The U.S. Coast Guard / by Carrie A. Braulick.
    p. cm.—(Blazers—the U.S. Armed Forces)
    Includes bibliographical references and index.
    ISBN 0-7368-3796-5 (hardcover)
    1. United States. Coast Guard—Juvenile literature. I. Title. II. Series.
VG53.B73 2005
363.28'6'0973—dc22   2004010536

Summary: Describes the U.S. Coast Guard, including its members, vehicles,
and missions.

Credits
Juliette Peters, set designer; Enoch Peterson and Steve Christensen, book
    designers; Jo Miller, photo researcher; Scott Thoms, photo editor

Photo Credits
DVIC/OS2 John Bouvia, 11; PA2 Telfair H. Brown, 27; PHAN Milne, 16–17;
    Tech. Sgt. Jose Hernandez, 12
Folio Inc./Ed Castle, cover (background); 13 (bottom)
Photo by Ted Carlson/Fotodynamics, 15, 28–29
U.S. Army Photo/Joseph Bonet, 20 (top)
U.S. Coast Guard Photo, 5, 8, 25; CW02 Alvin Dalmida Jr., 26; Larry Kellis,
    13 (top); PA1 Sarah Foster-Snell, cover (foreground), 20 (bottom); PA1
    Tom Sperduto, 14, 23; PA2 Matthew Belson, 19; PA2 Mike Hvozda, 22;
    PA3 Eric Hedaa, 7

**Capstone Press thanks members of the U.S. Coast Guard for their
assistance in preparing this book.**

1 2 3 4 5 6 10 09 08 07 06 05

Table of Contents

The U.S. Coast Guard in Action

A Coast Guard crew is on patrol. A crew member looks into binoculars. She sees people who need help.

The crew members get
into a small boat. They
speed over to the people.

The Coast Guard crew completes the rescue. The mission is a success.

BLAZER FACT

The Coast Guard goes on about 100 search and rescue missions each day.

Coast Guard Vehicles

The Coast Guard has many boats. Large cutters patrol in deep ocean areas.

Cutter

Icebreaker

Icebreakers break up ice so ships can pass through icy waterways. Crews use motor lifeboats for rescues in bad weather.

Motor lifeboat

Rigid hull inflatable boat

BLAZER FACT

Rigid hull inflatable boats can be lowered from Coast Guard cutters.

13

HH-60 Jayhawk

The HH-65 Dolphin helicopter hovers in place during rescues. The powerful HH-60 Jayhawk helicopter reaches mission areas quickly.

Cutter Diagram

Bridge

Bow

725

U.S. COA

Hull

GUARD

Deck

Stern

726

Weapons and Equipment

Aircraft have cables to lower rescue swimmers into the water. Rescue swimmers wear wet suits and flippers.

Rescue swimmer

★★★★★★★★★★★★

19

Coast Guard boats have weapons. The weapons help crews stop people who break laws.

Coast Guard stations have radar screens. The screens show boat locations. Coast Guard members use cell phones to talk to each other.

Coast Guard Jobs

Many Coast Guard members patrol the oceans on boats. Others fix vehicles or keep track of supplies.

The Coast Guard carries out missions on short notice. Members are ready to spring into action at any time.

BLAZER FACT

Each year, the Coast Guard seizes illegal drugs worth about $4 billion.

Coast Guard Ranks

★ ★ ★ ★ ★ ★ ★ ★ ★ ★ ★ ★ ★ ★ ★ ★

ENLISTED	OFFICERS
Seaman	Ensign
Petty Officer	Lieutenant
Chief Petty Officer	Commander
Master Chief Petty Officer	Captain
	Admiral

Coast Guard on a chase

29

Glossary

binoculars (buh-NOK-yuh-lurz)—a tool that makes distant objects appear closer

cutter (KUHT-uhr)—a large Coast Guard patrol boat

hover (HUHV-ur)—to remain in one place in the air

mission (MISH-uhn)—a military task

patrol (puh-TROHL)—to protect and watch an area

radar screen (RAY-dar SKREEN)—a screen that shows the location of objects after radar finds them

seize (SEEZ)—to take something by force

weapon (WEP-uhn)—something that can be used in a fight to attack or defend

wet suit (WET SOOT)—a close-fitting suit made of material that keeps divers warm in cold water

Read More

Cooper, Jason. *U.S. Coast Guard.* Fighting Forces. Vero Beach, Fla.: Rourke, 2004.

Holden, Henry M. *Coast Guard Rescue and Patrol Aircraft.* Aircraft. Berkeley Heights, N.J.: Enslow, 2002.

Lurch, Bruno. *United States Coast Guard.* U.S. Armed Forces. Chicago: Heinemann, 2004.

Internet Sites

FactHound offers a safe, fun way to find Internet sites related to this book. All of the sites on FactHound have been researched by our staff.

Here's how:

1. Visit *www.facthound.com*
2. Type in this special code **0736837965** for age-appropriate sites. Or enter a search word related to this book for a more general search.
3. Click on the **Fetch It** button.

FactHound will fetch the best sites for you!

Index